This book belongs to:

....

Copyright © 2021 Catherine Kwon All rights reserved.

No part of this publication may be reproduced, distributed, or trasmitted in any form or by any means, including photocopying, recording, or other electronic or mechanical methods, without the prior written permission of the creator, except in the case of brief quotations embodied in reviews and certain other non-commercial uses permitted by copyright law.

ㄱ makes a g sound, as in good

ㄱ [g]

고양이 (cat)

[go yang i]

Trace the lines

Color the image and trace its Korean name

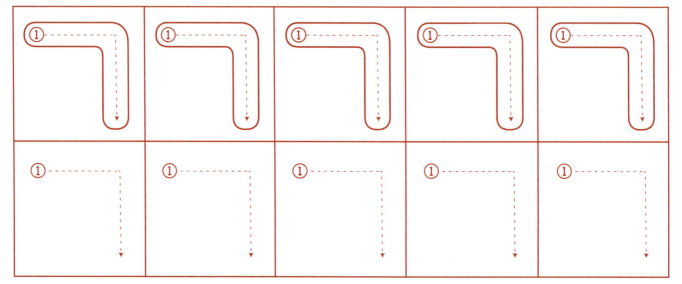

puppy

강	아	지
gang	a	ji
강	아	지
강	아	지

ㄴ makes a n sound, as in nice

ㄴ [n]

나무 (tree)

[na mu]

Trace the lines

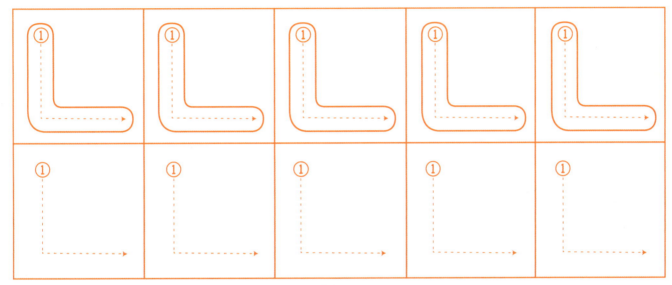

Color the image and trace its Korean name

butterfly

나	비
na	bi

나비

나비

ㄷ makes a **d** sound, as in **d**ragon

ㄷ [d]

달 (moon)

[dal]

Trace the lines

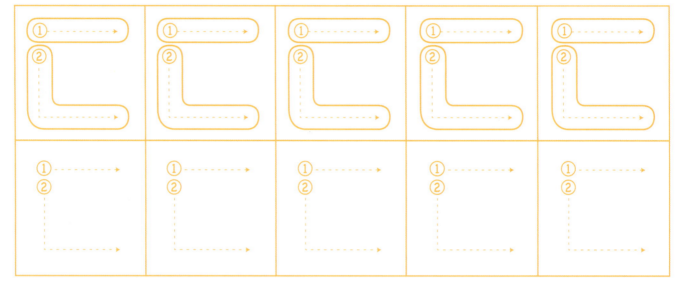

Color the image and trace its Korean name

carrot

당근

dang　geun

ㄹ makes a l/r sound, as in **l**emon or **r**obot

ㄹ [l/r]

레몬 (lemon)

[le mon]

Trace the lines

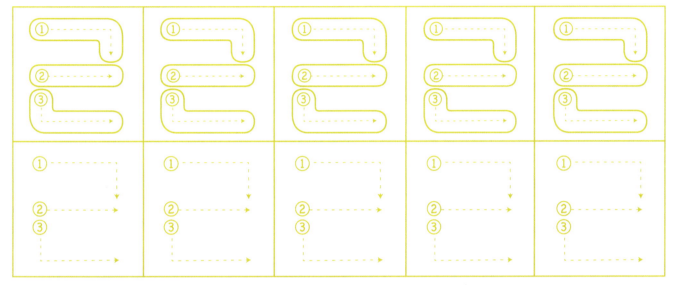

Color the image and trace its Korean name

robot

로	봇
ro	bot
로	봇
로	봇

5

Trace the lines

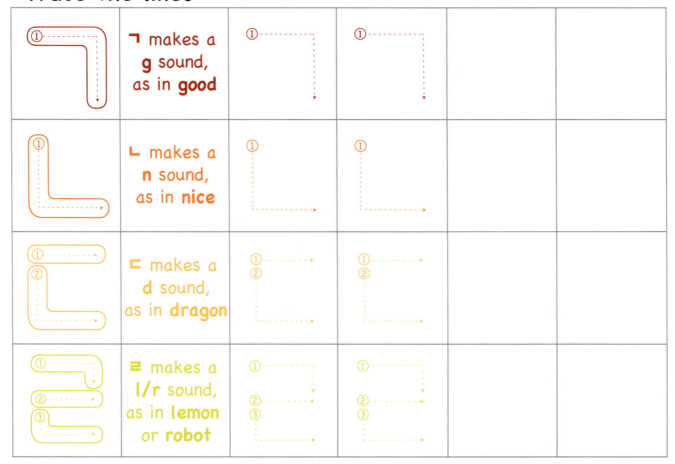

Draw a line to match the Korean alphabets sound.

[d] [l/r] [g] [n]

ㅁ makes a **m** sound, as in **m**ouse

문어 (octopus)

[**m**un eo]

Trace the lines

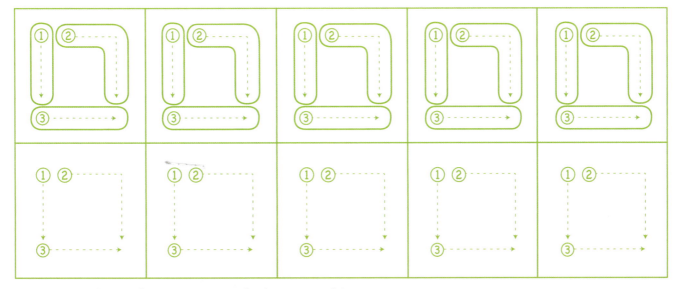

Color the image and trace its Korean name

hat

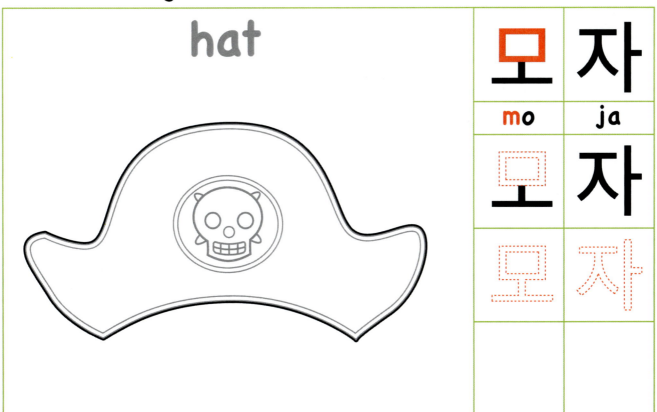

모	자
mo	ja
모	자
모	자

7

ㅂ makes a **b** sound, as in **b**rave

ㅂ [b]

바나나 (banana)

[**b**a na na]

Trace the lines

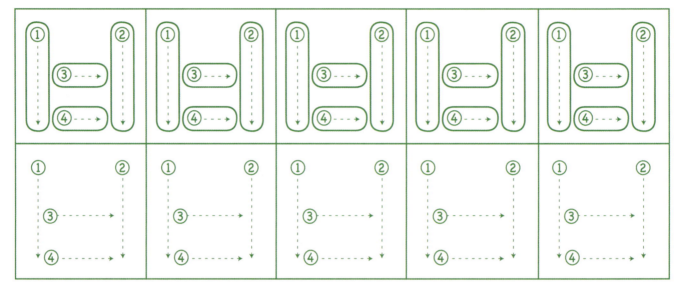

Color the image and trace its Korean name

ship

배
bae

8

ㅅ makes a **s** sound, as in **s**ea

ㅅ [s]

새 (bird)

[**s**ae]

Trace the lines

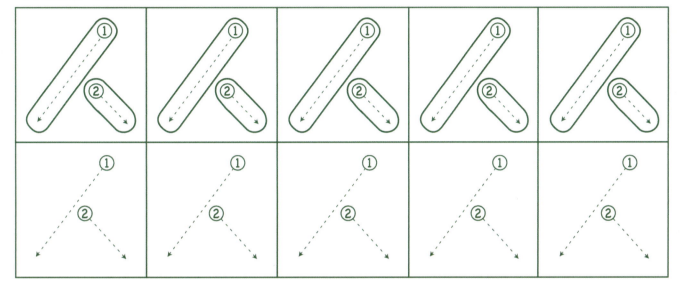

Color the image and trace its Korean name

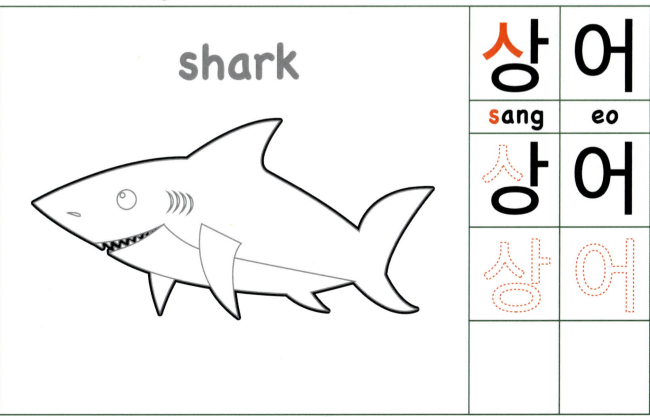

shark

상어
sang eo

Trace the lines

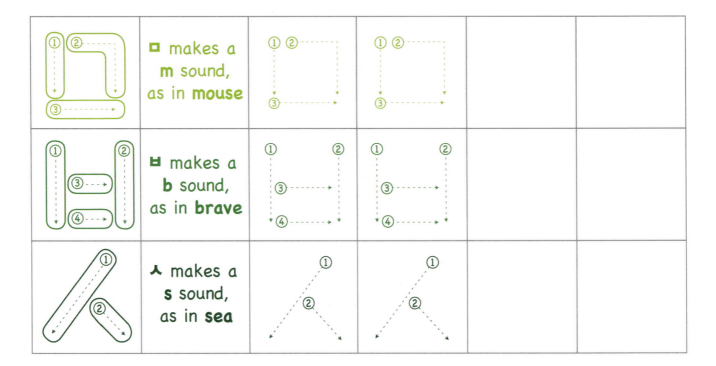

Draw a line to match the Korean alphabets sound

Trace the letters

	ㅏ	ㅑ	ㅓ	ㅕ	ㅗ
ㄱ	가	갸	거	겨	고
ㄴ	나	냐	너	녀	노
ㄷ	다	댜	더	뎌	도
ㄹ	라	랴	러	려	로
ㅁ	마	먀	머	며	모
ㅂ	바	뱌	버	벼	보
ㅅ	사	샤	서	셔	소

Trace the letters

	ㅛ	ㅜ	ㅠ	ㅡ	ㅣ
ㄱ	쿄	구	규	그	기
ㄴ	뇨	누	뉴	느	니
ㄷ	됴	두	듀	드	디
ㄹ	료	루	류	르	리
ㅁ	묘	무	뮤	므	미
ㅂ	뵤	부	뷰	브	비
ㅅ	쇼	수	슈	스	시

ㅇ makes no sound or a **-ng** sound, as in ki**ng**

[silent /-ng]

양 (sheep)

[ya**ng**]
silent ㅇ

Trace the lines

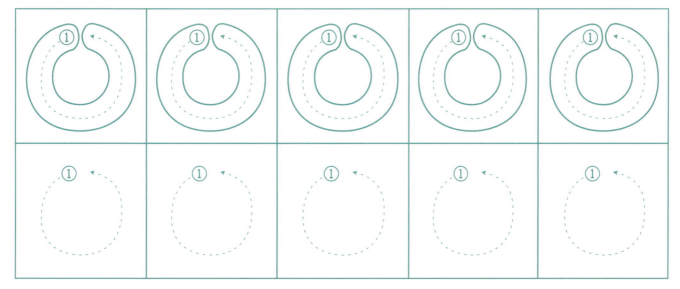

Color the image and trace its Korean name

child

아 이
silent ㅇ a | silent ㅇ i

13

ㅈ makes a j sound, as in joy

ㅈ [j]

자두 (plum)
[ja du]

Trace the lines

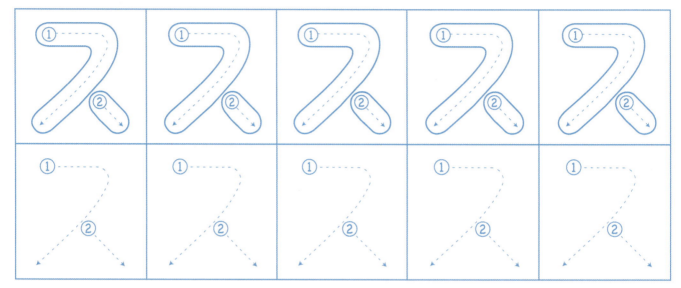

Color the image and trace its Korean name

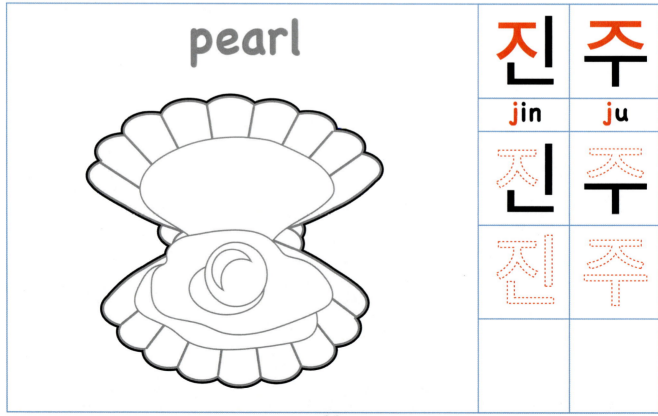

pearl

진 주
jin ju

ㅊ makes a ch sound, as in cheese

ㅊ [ch]

치즈 (cheese)

[chi jeu]

Trace the lines

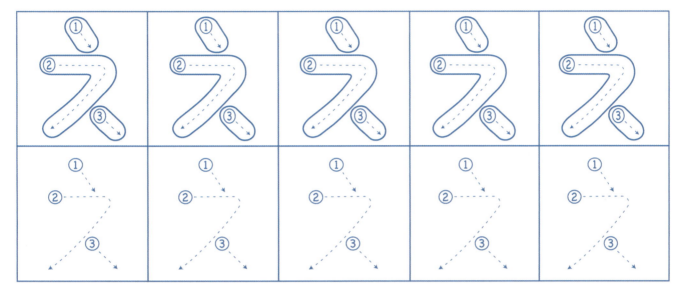

Color the image and trace its Korean name

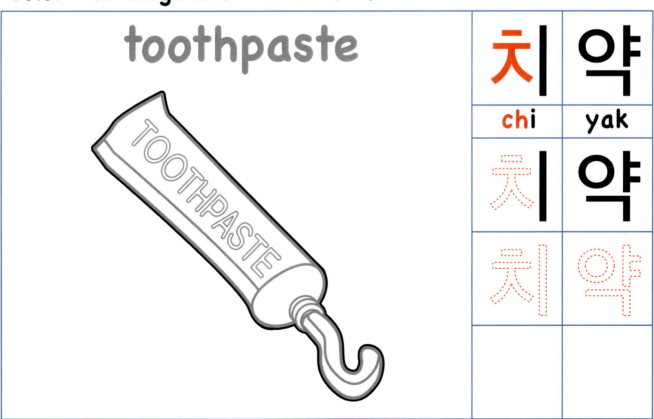

toothpaste

치	약
chi	yak
치	약
치	약

Trace the line

ㅇ	ㅇ makes no sound or a -ng sound, as in **king**	ㅇ	ㅇ		
ㅈ	ㅈ makes a j sound, as in **joy**	ㅈ	ㅈ		
ㅊ	ㅊ makes a ch sound, as in **cheese**	ㅊ	ㅊ		

Draw a line to match the Korean alphabets sound.

ㅋ makes a k sound, as in kind

ㅋ [k]

쿠키 (cookie)

[ku ki]

Trace the lines

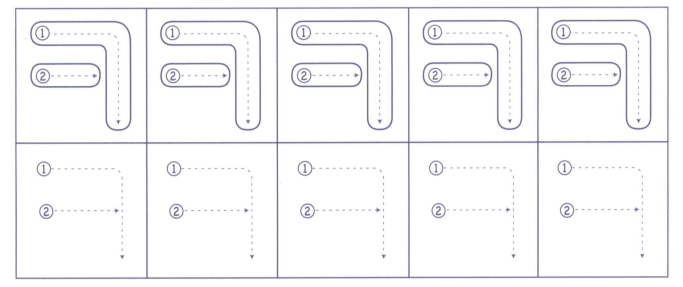

Color the image and trace its Korean name

camera

카 메 라
ka me ra

카 메 라

카 메 라

ㅌ makes a t sound, as in tomato

ㅌ [t]

토끼 (rabbit)

[to kki]

Trace the lines

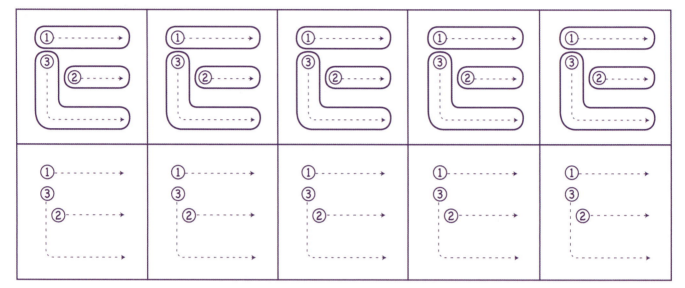

Color the image and trace its Korean name

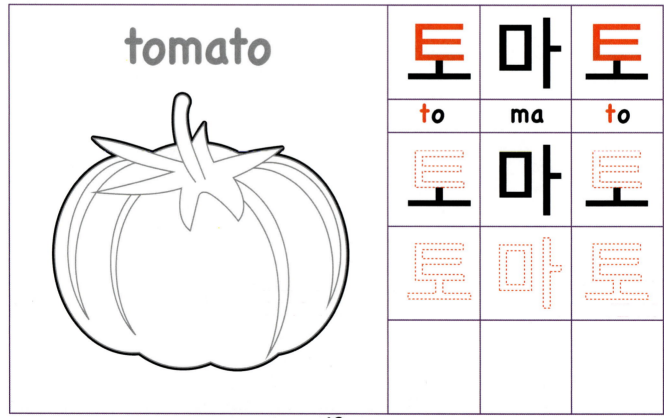

tomato

| 토 | 마 | 토 |
| to | ma | to |

ㅍ makes a **p** sound, as in **p**lease

ㅍ [p]

포크 (fork)
[**p**o keu]

Trace the lines

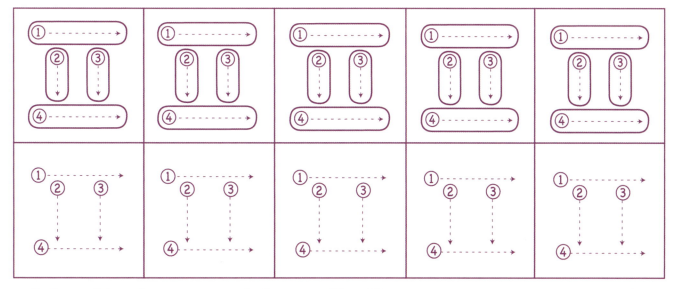

Color the image and trace its Korean name

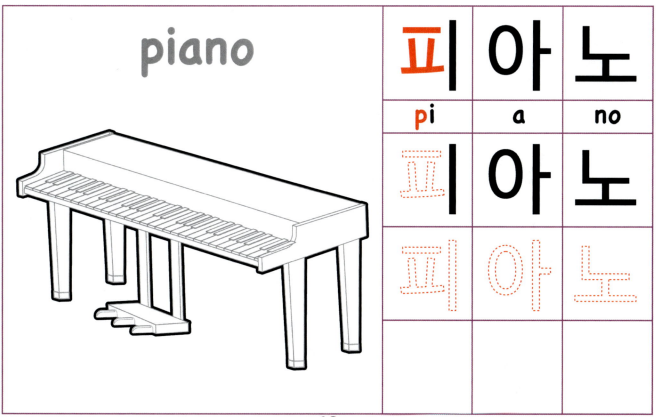

piano

피	아	노
pi	a	no
피	아	노
피	아	노

ㅎ makes a **h** sound, as in **h**appy

ㅎ [h]

해마 (sea horse)

[hae ma]

Trace the lines

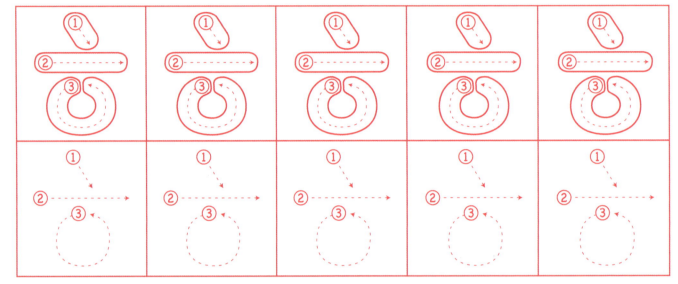

Color the image and trace its Korean name

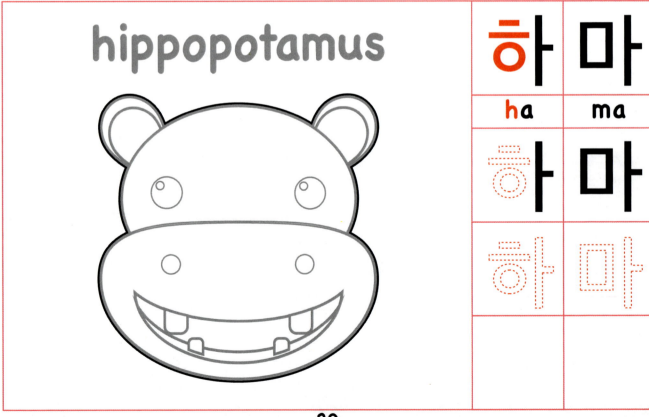

hippopotamus

하 마
ha ma

20

Trace the line

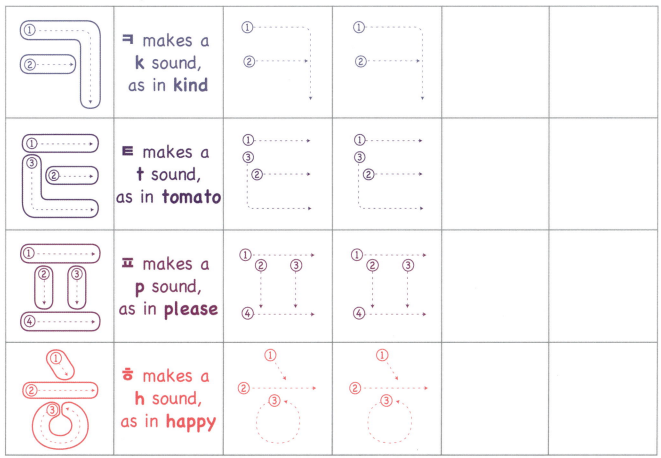

Draw a line to match the Korean alphabets sound.

Trace the letters

	ㅏ	ㅑ	ㅓ	ㅕ	ㅗ
ㅇ	아	야	어	여	오
ㅈ	자	쟈	저	져	조
ㅊ	차	챠	처	쳐	초
ㅋ	카	캬	커	켜	코
ㅌ	타	탸	터	텨	토
ㅍ	파	퍄	퍼	펴	포
ㅎ	하	햐	허	혀	호

Trace the letters

	ㅛ	ㅜ	ㅠ	ㅡ	ㅣ
ㅇ	요	우	유	으	이
ㅈ	죠	주	쥬	즈	지
ㅊ	쵸	추	츄	츠	치
ㅋ	쿄	쿠	큐	크	키
ㅌ	툐	투	튜	트	티
ㅍ	표	푸	퓨	프	피
ㅎ	효	후	휴	흐	히

ㅏ makes an **a** sound, as in f**a**ther

ㅏ [**a**]

아이 (child)

[**a** i]

Trace the lines

Color the image and trace its Korean name

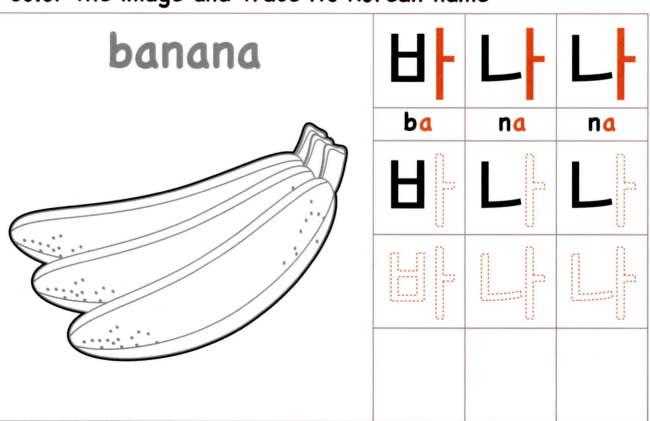

banana

바	나	나
b**a**	n**a**	n**a**

ㅑ makes a **ya** sound, as in **ya**hoo

ㅑ [ya]

야구공 (baseboll)

[**ya** goo gong]

Trace the lines

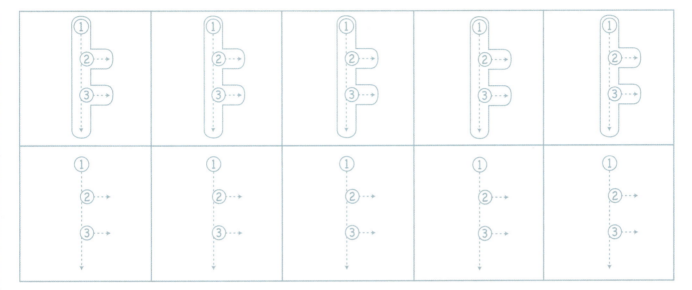

Color the image and trace its Korean name

sheep

양
yang

25

ㅓ makes a **eo** sound, as in **ea**rth

ㅓ [**eo**]

섬 (island)

[s**eo**m]

Trace the lines

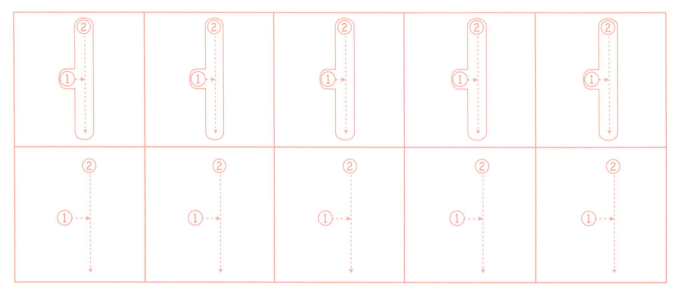

Color the image and trace its Korean name

alligator

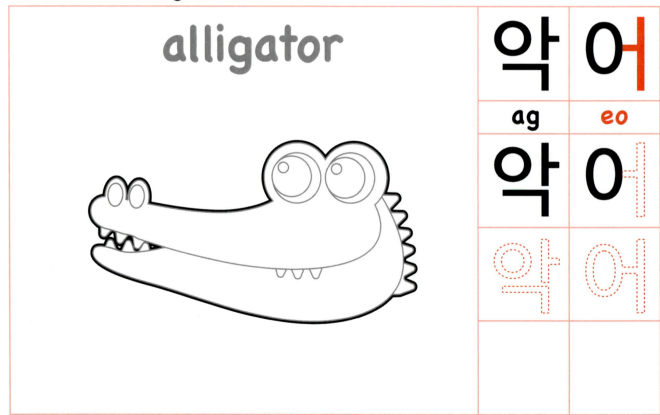

악 어
ag **eo**

ㅕ makes a **yeo** sound, as in yo**u**ng

ㅕ [yeo]

병아리 (chick)
[b**yeo**ng a ri]

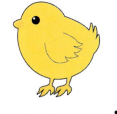

Trace the lines

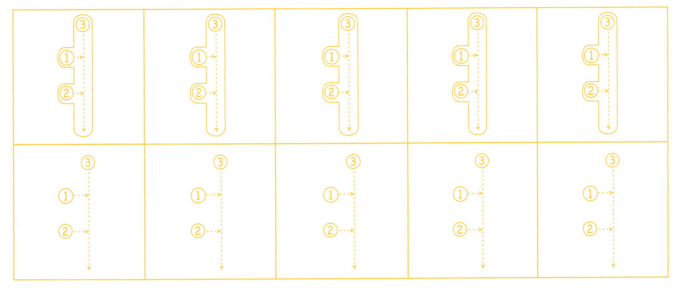

Color the image and trace its Korean name

fox

여 우
yeo oo

27

ㅗ makes a **o** sound, as in **oh**

ㅗ [o]

농구공 (basketball)

[n**o**ng goo g**o**ng]

Trace the lines

Color the image and trace its Korean name

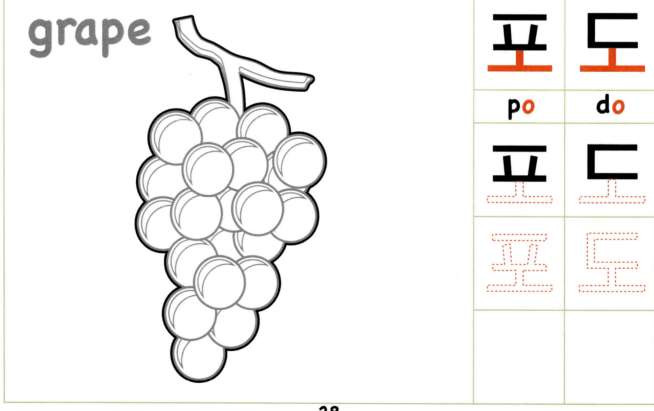

grape

포	도
p**o**	d**o**
포	도

ㅛ makes a yo sound, as in yo-yo

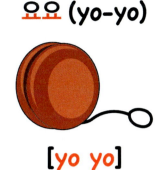

요요 (yo-yo)

[yo yo]

Trace the lines

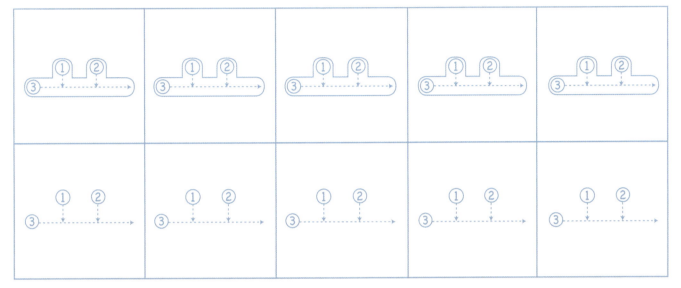

Color the image and trace its Korean name

dragon

yong

ㅜ makes a **oo** sound, as in z**oo**

ㅜ [oo]

옥수수 (corn)
[ok soo soo]

Trace the lines

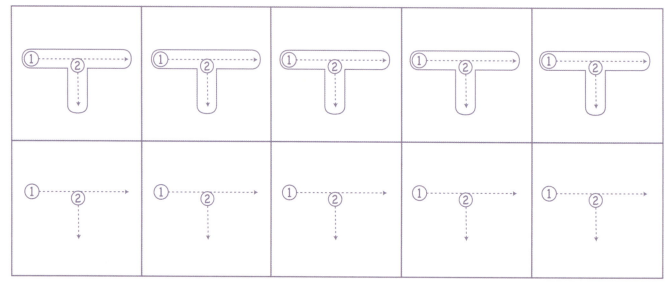

Color the image and trace its Korean name

milk

우	유
oo	you
우	유
우	유

ㅠ makes a you sound, as in you

ㅠ [you]

굴 (tangerine)

[gyoul]

Trace the lines

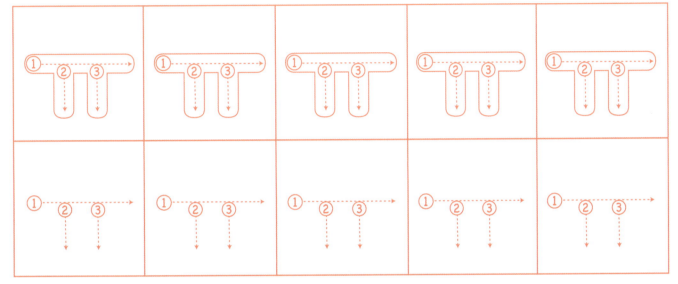

Color the image and trace its Korean name

tube

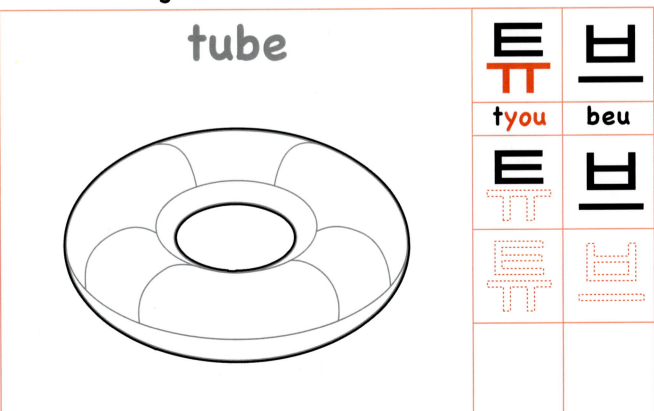

튜	브
tyou	beu
트	브
ㅠ	ㅡ
트	브
ㅠ	ㅡ

— makes a **eu** sound, as in brok**e**n or butt**o**n

당근 (carrot)

[dang g**eu**n]

Trace the lines

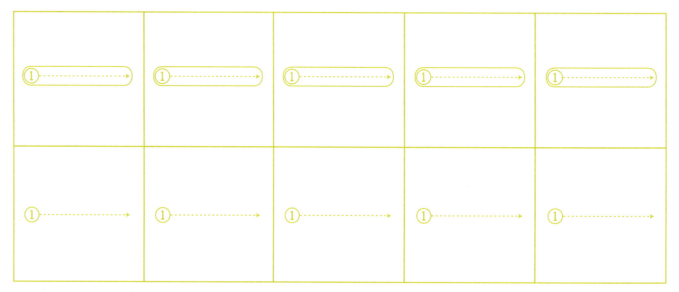

Color the image and trace its Korean name

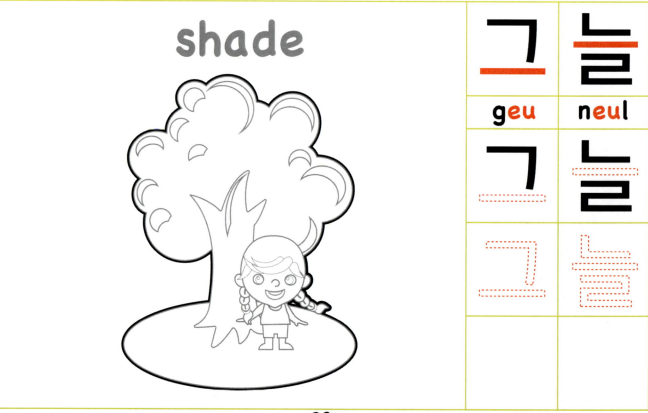

shade

geu | neul

32

I makes a i/ee sound, as in ski or cheese

ㅣ [i/ee]

비 (rain)
[bi]

Trace the lines

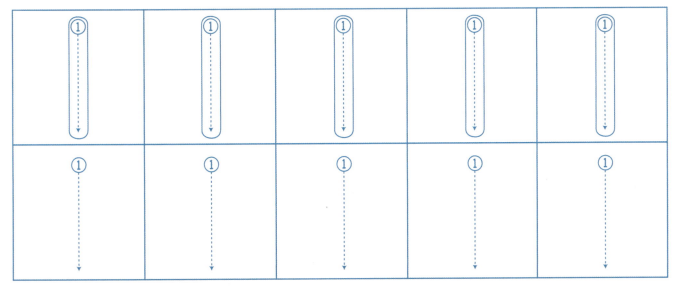

Color the image and trace its Korean name

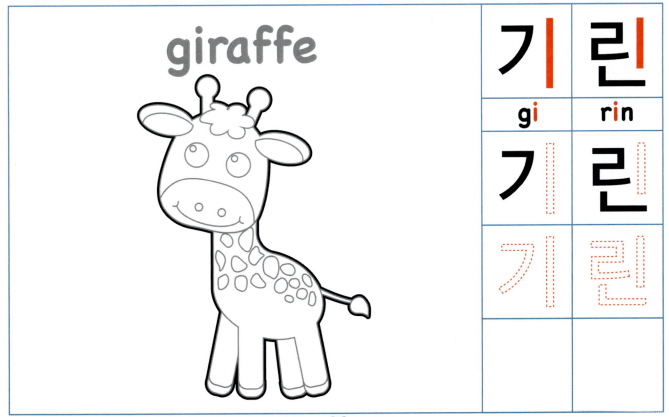

giraffe

기 린
gi rin

33

Trace the line

ㅏ	ㅏ makes an **a** sound, as in **father**				
ㅑ	ㅑ makes a **ya** sound, as in **yahoo**				
ㅓ	ㅓ makes a **eo** sound, as in **earth**				
ㅕ	ㅕ makes a **yeo** sound, as in **young**				
ㅗ	ㅗ makes a **o** sound, as in **oh**				

Draw a line to match the Korean alphabets sound.

ㅏ   ㅑ   ㅓ   ㅕ   ㅗ

[eo]   [a]   [ya]   [o] [yeo]

Trace the line

ㅛ	ㅛ makes a yo sound, as in yo-yo				
ㅜ	ㅜ makes a oo sound, as in zoo				
ㅠ	ㅠ makes a you sound, as in you				
ㅡ	ㅡ makes a eu sound, as in broken or button				
ㅣ	ㅣ makes a i/ee sound, as in ski or cheese				

Draw a line to match the Korean alphabets sound.

ㅛ   ㅜ   ㅠ   ㅡ   ㅣ

[yo] [you] [ee] [eu] [oo]

Trace the letters

	ㅏ	ㅑ	ㅓ	ㅕ	ㅗ
ㄱ					
ㄴ					
ㄷ					
ㄹ					
ㅁ					
ㅂ					
ㅅ					

Trace the letters

	ㅛ	ㅜ	ㅠ	ㅡ	ㅣ
ㄱ					
ㄴ					
ㄷ					
ㄹ					
ㅁ					
ㅂ					
ㅅ					

Trace the letters

	ㅏ	ㅑ	ㅓ	ㅕ	ㅗ
ㅇ					
ㅈ					
ㅊ					
ㅋ					
ㅌ					
ㅍ					
ㅎ					

Trace the letters

	ㅛ	ㅜ	ㅠ	ㅡ	ㅣ
ㅇ					
ㅈ					
ㅊ					
ㅋ					
ㅌ					
ㅍ					
ㅎ					

CERTIFICATE
of COMPLETION

AWARDED TO

For Completion of
Basic Korean Alphabet

Name: _____

Signed: *Lil's Pirates*   Date: _____

Made in the USA
Coppell, TX
11 May 2025